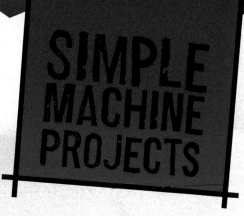

SIMPLE MACHINE PROJECTS

Making Machines
with
Ramps
and
Wedges

Chris Oxlade

raintree

a Capstone company — publishers for children

Raintree is an imprint of Capstone Global Library Limited, a company incorporated in England and Wales having its registered office at 7 Pilgrim Street, London, EC4V 6LB – Registered company number: 6695582

www.raintree.co.uk
myorders@raintree.co.uk

Edited by James Benefield and Erika Shores
Designed by Steve Mead
Original illustrations © Capstone Global Library Ltd 2015
Picture research by Jo Miller
Production by Victoria Fitzgerald
Originated by Capstone Global Library Ltd
Printed and bound in China

ISBN 978 1 406 28928 2
18 17 16 15 14
10 9 8 7 6 5 4 3 2 1

British Library Cataloguing in Publication Data
A full catalogue record for this book is available from the British Library.

Acknowledgements
We would like to thank the following for permission to reproduce photographs: All photos Capstone Studio: Karon Dubke except: Courtesy of Lockheed Martin, 12; Dreamstime: Douglas Greenwald, 19, Frankljunior, 29 (bottom), Gary Telford, 10, Tsomka, 18, Vladimir Melnik, 17; iStockphotos: Huntstock_Images, 4; Robert Harding: National Geographic/Nick Norman, 13; Science Source: Tony Freeman, 7; Shutterstock: Arkady Ten, 27, Christina Richards, 16, Dan Breckwoldt, 25, Florence McGinn, 26, holbox, 29 (top), jps, 24.

Design Elements: Shutterstock: Timo Kohlbacher.

We would like to thank Harold Pratt and Richard Taylor for their invaluable help in the preparation of this book.

Every effort has been made to contact copyright holders of material reproduced in this book. Any omissions will be rectified in subsequent printings if notice is given to the publisher.

All the internet addresses (URLs) given in this book were valid at the time of going to press. However, due to the dynamic nature of the internet, some addresses may have changed, or sites may have changed or ceased to exist since publication. While the author and publisher regret any inconvenience this may cause readers, no responsibility for any such changes can be accepted by either the author or the publisher.

CONTENTS

Some words are shown in bold, **like this**. You can find out what they mean by looking in the glossary.

WHAT ARE RAMPS AND WEDGES?

You must have walked up a slope into a building or over a bridge, put a doorstop under a door, cut your food with a knife or used a zip. Then **ramps** and **wedges** have helped you, because slopes are ramps and knifes and zips use wedges to work. In this book, you'll see many examples of ramps and wedges, and the projects will help you to understand how ramps and wedges work.

A wheelchair ramp allows people in wheelchairs to push themselves up into buildings.

SIMPLE MACHINES

Ramps and wedges are similar to each other. They are one of the five types of simple machines. The other four are the **pulley**, the **wheel and axle**, the **lever** and the **screw**. Also, **springs** are like simple machines. Simple machines help us to do jobs, such as moving heavy loads, and breaking and cutting materials.

ramp

wedge

A wedge is like two ramps on top of one another.

What other uses are there for ramps and wedges?

HOW WEDGES WORK

A wedge is a very simple machine indeed! It is a piece of hard material, such as wood, plastic or rubber. It is thick at one end and thin at the other, like a slice of pie. When you push a wedge between two objects, the wedge pushes the objects apart.

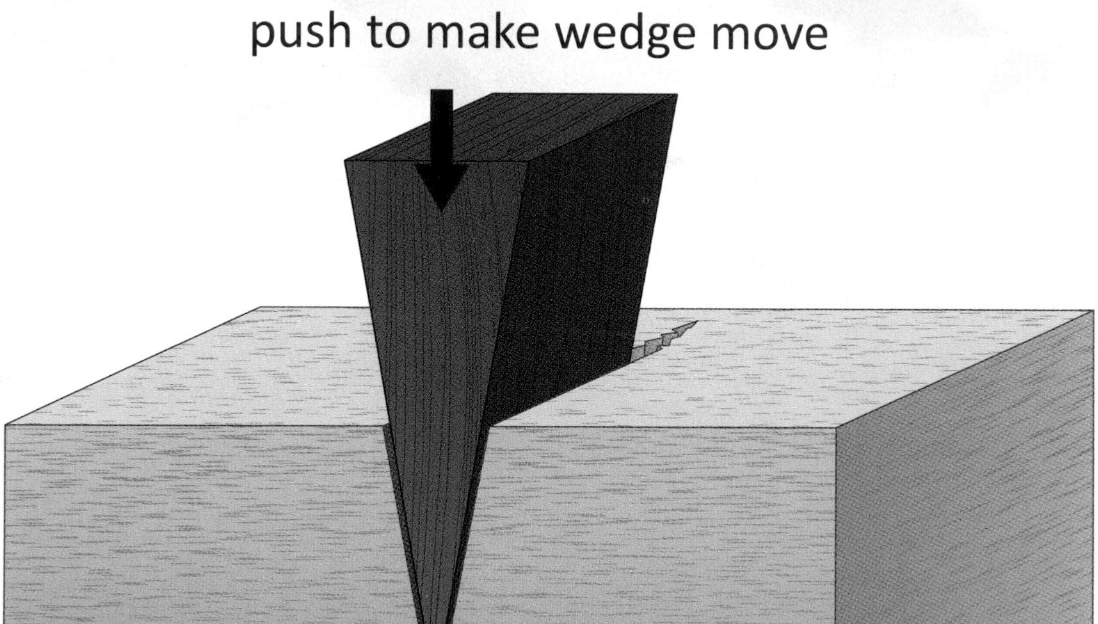

push to make wedge move

push made by wedge

A wedge makes a sideways push as you push it into a material.

It's the shape of the wedge that does the pushing. It changes the direction of the **force** (see panel below) you make, and makes the push larger. A wedge can also jam things in place. For example, you put a door wedge under a door to stop the door from closing.

An axe head has a wedge. It cuts into wood and splits the wood apart with its wedge-shaped blade.

FORCE AND MOTION

Simple machines such as wedges can change force (a push or a pull) and **motion** (movement). A simple machine can make a force larger or smaller, or change its direction. A simple machine can also make a motion larger or smaller, or change its direction.

The power of wedges

This project shows how a wedge can make a force much larger.

1 Carefully fill the boxes with the books to make the boxes heavy.

2 Put the boxes next to one another on the floor.

3 Place the wedge on its edge, with its narrow end just in the gap between the boxes (see below).

STEP 3

4 Push the wedge slowly into the gap. What happens to the boxes?

5 Put a box against a wall and put the narrow end of the wedge under the edge.

6 Slowly push the wedge under the box.

STEP 5

STEP 6

What did you find out?

Think about how easy it was to move the boxes apart with and without the wedge. The wedge makes it much easier because it makes the push you give much larger.

SHARP AND BLUNT

All wedges have two sides. The angle between the two sides is important for how a wedge works. Some wedges have a small angle between their two sides, and some have a wider angle. Sharp wedges have a smaller angle and look narrow.

A narrow wedge makes a larger sideways push than a wide wedge. So a narrow wedge is easier to push into a material. That is why needles and pins, which you push in with your fingers, must be very sharp.

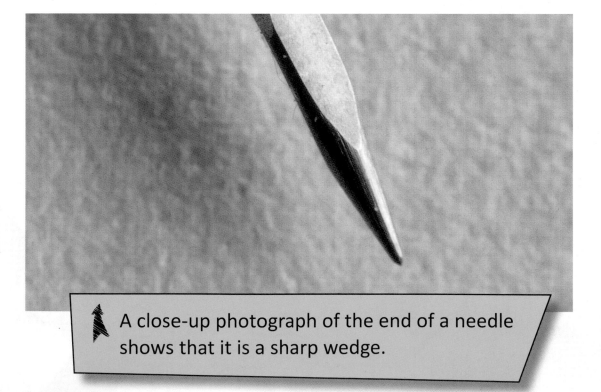

A close-up photograph of the end of a needle shows that it is a sharp wedge.

MAKING HOLES

For this mini project, you'll need some modelling clay, a pencil and a tray.

❶ Put the clay on a tray to protect your work surface. Flatten out the clay.

❷ Gently push the blunt, unsharpened end of the pencil into the clay (see picture below).

STEP 2

❸ Turn the pencil over and gently push the sharp, pointy end into the clay.

The sharp end of the pencil went into the clay more easily because it is a narrow wedge.

MOVING MATERIALS

Imagine a ship that is moving quickly through water (or look at the photo below). What shape is the ship's **bow**? What's happening to the water?

You should see that the bow is a wedge. The ship's engines push the ship forwards and the bow pushes the water to the sides. The wedge is moving the water. Moving materials like this is another job that wedges can do for us.

wedge-shaped bow

A ship's bow is a wedge that pushes water aside as the ship moves along.

Another example of a wedge moving materials is the wedge on a snowplough. It has a wedge-shaped blade that pushes snow to the side of a road or railway line.

A snowplough on a truck can clear deep snow from a road.

MOVING THROUGH THE AIR

High-speed planes and express trains have wedge-shaped fronts. These wedge-shaped fronts push the air aside as the planes and trains speed along.

Pushing air aside

Try this project to find out why aircraft and express trains have wedge-shaped noses.

What you need:
- some thin card
- scissors
- ruler
- sticky tape
- hairdryer

1 Using the thin card, cut out two rectangles 10 cm x 18 cm, two squares 10 cm x 10 cm and one rectangle 10 cm x 12 cm.

2 Get the two 10 x 18 cm shapes. Measure four equal sections, lengthways, and fold (see picture).

STEP 2

3 Tape the edges together to make cuboid shapes.

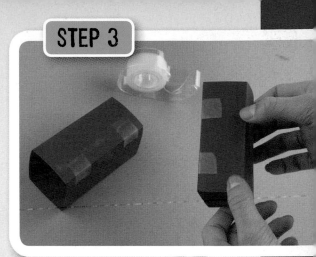

STEP 3

4 Get the 12 cm x 10 cm rectangle. Measure it into three equal parts, lengthways. Fold and stick along the lines to form a wedge shape.

STEP 5

5 Stick the shapes to the 10 x 10 cm square bases.

6 Stand the shapes on the worktop. Hold the hairdryer about a metre in front of them. Put it on a low setting. Slowly move it towards the models.

STEP 6

What did you find out?
The hairdryer will get close to the wedge-shaped tube before it moves. How does it compare to what happens with the other shape?

HOW RAMPS WORK

Scientists call a ramp an inclined plane. That means a flat surface that is tilted up – one end is higher than the other (a slope). It is easier to push or pull something up a ramp than it is to lift it straight up.

Ramps are used on building sites. Builders put up ramps to move wheelbarrows full of heavy materials up or down. Ramps used to load lorries work in the same way.

A ramp makes moving heavy machinery a lot easier.

It might mean a longer route, but this series of gentle ramps is kinder on your car.

Obvious (and not so obvious...) ramps

Ramps are all over the place! As we have seen, there are obvious ones to see, such as loading ramps on lorries and ships.

There are also many that are not obvious, such as zigzag paths and roads. Roads going up mountains are a series of gentle ramps. Most vehicles (and people!) would have problems getting up a steep slope on a mountainside.

GOING DOWN RAMPS

Ramps are useful for lowering heavy objects. Think about unloading a lorry. It's much easier to slide a heavy box down a ramp than it is to lift it straight down. The force needed to stop it sliding down the ramp is small. It's smaller than the force you need to stop the box from falling straight down.

Falling to the ground

A ramp slows how quickly things fall. On a slide, you get to the ground more slowly than if you had fallen. That's because a slide is a ramp. The force of gravity pulls you down, but the slide makes the force on you smaller.

A water slide is a simple ramp that lets you go downhill fast without falling.

RIDING THE RAMPS

Roller coasters use ramps to control the speed of the cars. A ramp carries the cars to the top of the first drop. Steep downward sections of track make cars speed up quickly, and steep uphill sections of track make them slow down quickly.

Moving up ramps

Try this project to see how a ramp reduces the force you need to hold up an object.

1 Cut a piece of thick card about 20 cm x 6 cm. Cut two short slots in one end of the card, about 1 cm long, and about 1 cm apart.

What you need:
- some thick card
- a thin elastic band about 10 cm long
- a paper clip
- medium-sized metal model car
- a piece of thick wood (see step 7)
- some smaller books
- a pen
- string

STEP 1

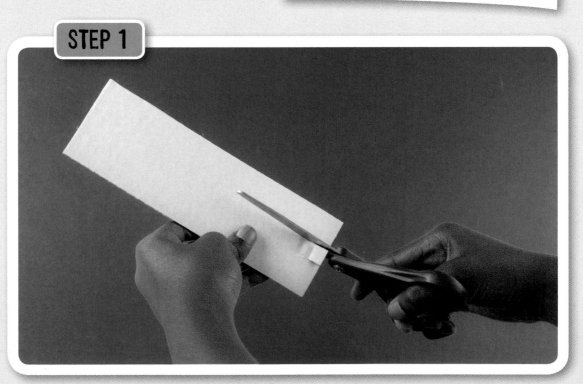

2 Push one end of the elastic band onto the slots so that the band is hooked around the back of the card.

3 Slightly unbend the paper clip and slide it onto the free end of the elastic band to make a hook.

4 Pull very gently down on the paper clip, just hard enough to make the elastic band straight. Draw a line level with the end of the band.

STEP 4

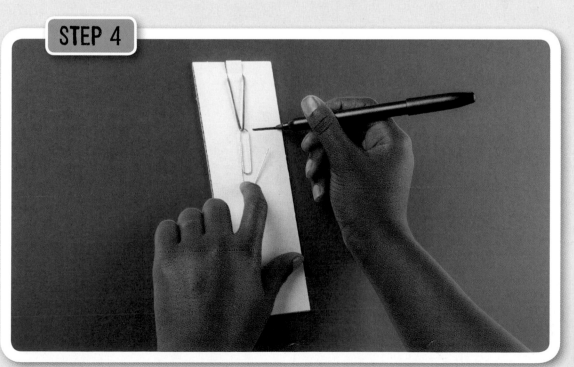

Measure and cut a piece of string about 5 to 10 cm long. Tie a loop in one end of the string, and tie or tape the other end to the car. Put the loop of the string on the paper clip.

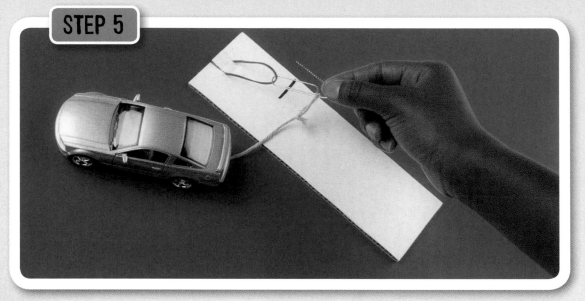

STEP 5

STEP 6

 Lift the card by its top end so that the car dangles from the elastic band. Mark the position of the end of the elastic band on the card.

7 Lean the piece of wood on the pile of the small books to make a steep plane. Put the car on the plane, facing down the plane (see below). How far does the elastic band stretch now?

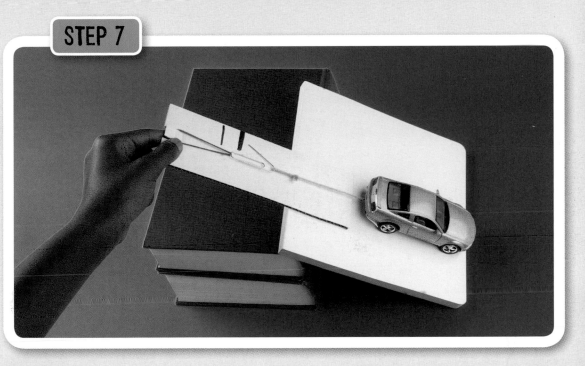

STEP 7

8 Now take away some of the smaller books so that the plane is less steep than before. How far does the elastic band stretch now?

What did you find out?

Did it take more force to support the car hanging in the air or the car resting on the ramp? The less steep you made the ramp, the smaller the force you needed.

RAMPS AND WEDGES IN HISTORY

Historical wedges

The very first man-made tools used wedges. For example, people made knives and axes by chipping stone such as **flint** to make sharp edges. Also, when people started growing crops, they used sticks as wedges to dig furrows in the soil to plant seeds.

Historical ramps

Thousands of years ago, people built stone monuments. But they had no construction machines to lift and move huge blocks. They must have used ramps to push or pull blocks by hand. Even a few hundred years ago, engineers built ramps to move things. Ramps moved railway wagons and canal boats up and down hills.

This stone axe was made around 7,000 years ago by chipping a piece of flint.

BUILDING PYRAMIDS

Experts think that the ancient Egyptians built colossal stone pyramids with the help of ramps. They may have built longer and longer ramps as the pyramids rose up, and then taken the ramps down at the end.

The famous pyramids at Giza, in Egypt, may have been built by dragging huge blocks of stone up earth ramps.

RAMPS AND WEDGES IN COMPLEX MACHINES

Complex machines are made up of simple machines working together. Many complicated machines contain ramps and wedges.

You have probably seen wedges working in construction machines. Diggers have wedges on their buckets that slice into the soil. Concrete-breaking machines have chisels with wedge-shaped tips to split concrete.

A construction digger has wedge-shaped teeth on its bucket for slicing into the soil.

Factories and mines often have ramps for moving materials from one place to another. The ramps have moving belts on them that pull the materials up the ramp. You can see similar ramps at airports. These ramps move baggage around, for example from the ground into the baggage holds of aircraft.

An airport baggage loader has a sloped conveyor belt to move heavy bags into an aircraft's hold.

ZIP WEDGES

Take a close look at a zip. You should be able to see a wedge at work. Inside the pull slider (the bit you pull to do up the zip), is a wedge that pulls the teeth of the zip apart as you undo the zip.

FACTS AND FUN

AMAZING RAMPS AND WEDGES

Like roads, some railways in mountainous areas of the world climb hills in a series of zigzags. Trains go backwards and forwards across the hillside, changing direction again and again.

The oldest tools ever found are simple stone cutting tools with sharp wedge-shaped edges. They were found in Ethiopia between 1992 and 1994 and were made over 2.5 million years ago.

Golfers carry a club (called a wedge) with a wedge-shaped head. When the club hits a ball, the wedge pushes the ball upwards as well as forwards, so the ball flies high in the air.

The Ronquières Inclined Plane, in Belgium, is a ramp that lifts canal boats up a hill. It is 1,432 metres (4,698 feet) long and 68 metres (223 feet) higher at one end than the other.

The world's longest water slide is more than 40 metres (131 feet) from top to bottom. Riders can reach speeds of more than 106 kilometres (66 miles) per hour.

ANCIENT MACHINES

The wedge is the oldest of all simple machines. Humans were chopping up food with wedge-shaped cutting tools nearly two million years ago. It's amazing that we are using wedges for the same job today.

Where are the ramps and wedges?

You've read in this book that ramps and wedges are everywhere. Look at these pictures to see for yourself.

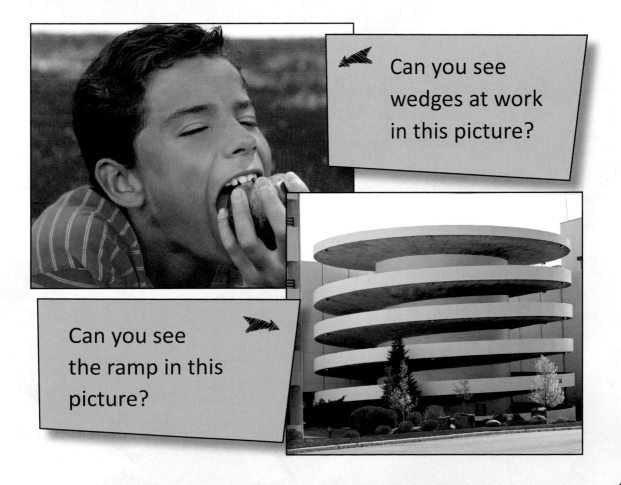

Can you see wedges at work in this picture?

Can you see the ramp in this picture?

GLOSSARY

bow sharp, front end of a ship or boat

flint hard, grey rock that splits into sharp pieces when it is hit hard

force push or a pull

lever long bar that is pushed or pulled against a fulcrum to help move heavy loads or cut material

motion movement

pulley simple machine made up of wheels and rope, used to lift or pull objects

ramp simple machine used to lift heavy objects

screw simple machine that has a spiral-shaped thread, used to fix or lift materials

spring device that can be pressed or pulled but returns to its first shape when released

wedge simple machine used to split apart materials

wheel and axle simple machine made up of a wheel on an axle, used to turn or lift objects

FIND OUT MORE

Books

Put Wedges to the Test, Sally M. Walker & Roseann Feldmann (Lerner Classroom, 2011)

Put Inclined Planes to the Test, Sally M. Walker & Roseann Feldmann (Lerner Classroom, 2011)

How Machines Work: The Interactive Guide to Simple Machines and Mechanisms, Nick Arnold (Running Press, 2011)

Websites

www.edheads.org/activities/simple-machines/index.shtml
Discover more about machines on this website.

www.engquest.org.au/students-sm-lp.cfm#Wheels?CFID=686982&CFTOKEN=57534071
On this website, you can learn about simple machines and how they work.

www.explainthatstuff.com/toolsmachines.html
This site has some useful diagrams to help explain all about simple machines.

Video

mocomi.com/wedge
This animation shows you how wedges work.

INDEX